TIMBER CURTAIN

FRANCES McCUE

Publisher:
Chin Music Press
1501 Pike Place, Suite 329
Seattle, WA 98101

www.chinmusicpress.com

ISBN: 978-1634059121

Library of Congress Cataloging-in-Publication Data

NAMES: McCue, Frances, author.

TITLE: Timber curtain / Frances McCue.

DESCRIPTION: Seattle : Chin Music Press Inc., 2017.

IDENTIFIERS:
LCCN 2017023918 (print)
LCCN 2017024115 (ebook)
ISBN 9781634059138
ISBN 1634059131
ISBN 9781634059121 (paperback)
ISBN 1634059123 (paperback)

LC record available at
https://lccn.loc.gov/2017023918

SUBJECTS:
BISAC: POETRY / American /
General.
LITERARY COLLECTIONS /
American / General.

CLASSIFICATION:
LCC PS3563.C35275 (ebook)
LCC PS3563.C35275 A6 2017 (print)
DDC 811/.54--dc23

First [1] Edition.

Cover and page design by Dan D Shafer.
Text set in Athelas and Folio.

Printed in Canada by Gauvin Press.

TIMBER CURTAIN

FRANCES McCUE

CHIN MUSIC
P R E S S

TABLE OF CONTENTS

At First   1
Timber Curtain   7
Unspooled...   9

I.

Along with the Dead Poet Richard Hugo   11
Gentrification Wedge   12
Call It an Interest   13
Cranes on the Skyline, Coming Toward Us   14
Retracing My Steps   15
Back to the Origins   16
To Conjure the Past Is to Beg the Future for More   17
The Mist Takes Hold   18
Along with ▮ Dead ▮ ▮ Hugo   19
▮ Wedge   21
Hugo Wedge   25

II.

What Happened There   27
Believe What You Will   30
Sightlines   33
For What It Was   34
One Artist's Beginnings   35
In the Whisper Gone, You Are a Little Girl   37

III.

Say You Come Here   41
Why Real Estate Is So Emotional   42
If You Really Want Urban Planning   43
If You Really Want ███ ███   45
The Measure of My Returns   48
Trying to Get By   50
Fixing in Place   51
Maybe This Building Should Go   52
Maybe This ███ Should Go   53
███ This ███ ███ █   57

IV.

Take the Old Dream   59
Even as It Rots, You Can't Move It   60
Old Talk about the West   61
Migration Hatred   62
Gratitude   64
Not Exactly   65
Consolation   67
███ sol █ o █   69
Monkey in Training   72
Art Monster   73
The Street Song Last on Everyone's Lips   75
Timber Curtain   77
Timber Curtain Redux   82
Heart of the Cedar   83
At the River Mouth   85
Practical   87
The Wind Up   88
███ ███ Up   90

V.

If Icebergs Were Ships 95
Cedar Theater 96
The Frontier Room 98
████ did you go█ ████ ███████? . 99
Where did you go, Kurt Cobain? 103
Good Intentions 105
A Word about Nostalgia 106
Another Way to See It 107
If Once My Cities Merged 108
Crossing Over the Crossing-Over Land 109
Old World Recovery 110
Living with Emergencies 111
The Panic Merchant 112
The ████ ██████ 114
Flattening Mortar 118
Flattening ████ 119
In the Small Time 122
I Am Still Looking Up to Find You 124
The Demolition: Before and After 125
The Reveal 128
Those We Left There 129
Fixing in Place with Curtains 131
Farewell Finally Hugo 132

Epilogue

The Once-Was Beginnings and Endings 135
The Wind Up in Façade 137
Shifting the Curtains in Place 139
Say You Come Here 141
████ ███ ████ Here 143
Say ████ ████ ████ 147

Notes

Notes 151
Acknowledgements 153

For Team Demo Hugo
who made the film Where the House Was,
the inspiration for this book.

For Richard Hugo House

For Linda Breneman, Linda Johnson, and Andrea Lewis,
who made certain it began and carried on.

"Every house I ever lived in was torn down."

Richard Hugo

AT FIRST

Once, I lived in a building that was named for a poet. It was the mid-90s through the turn of the millennium and that part of Seattle, Capitol Hill, was full of music, theaters, art spots, and some pretty cheap places to live.

My apartment was above a café where poets and writers and actors performed on stage. At night, you could hear the whoosh of applause below our floorboards. In my little girl's bedroom, she'd prattle herself to sleep with the sounds of poets singing each to each.

My husband, Gary, and I had our bedroom off of the back porch. We were happy there. We loved each other. Seattle was just the place for us—a city dimly lit but humming with intention. We felt like anything could happen.

Not long after we moved in, the World Trade Organization protests came. We marched downtown, and later, after we came home, the police pushed the protesters further into Capitol Hill. Outside our apartment, they were spraying tear gas and we put wet washcloths on Madeleine's face to keep her from breathing it in.

Our apartment had a red door. I'd shut it and go down the hall to work. My office overlooked a playfield. One day, a kid hit a baseball over the netting, through my window, and the ball bounced on the desk and rolled to the floor. It was a near miss: Maddy was playing underneath the desk and I felt like the ball was an omen of some kind.

We called the building Richard Hugo House. That was Gary's idea, I think. The building had once been a funeral home with a chapel. Afterwards, a couple of theaters took over, and by the time we moved in, we were starting a writers' center. It was my job to run the place.

Richard Hugo was from White Center, a bedraggled town off of the southwestern fringe of Seattle—not a likely place for a poet to come from. Our building, the one we named after him, was not one that Hugo himself had set foot in, unless he had come across town for a funeral there. Since Manning's Mortuary was a Catholic joint and Hugo's people were Methodists, I doubt it.

But what do I know? I was nineteen when Hugo died and I was living in the East. I never met him. What I glean of him is from his writing. And from having met his friends and family years later. I know that he loved baseball and ice cream. And booze and fishing.

Hugo was a Westerner. His poems were, at first, set in Seattle and around the Puget Sound. At the end of his life, he settled in Missoula, Montana, and a good number of his poems came out of that region. This bit of Hugo's history was important to us, the tie of the nascent literary center to the "true West" feeling of Montana where he wrote poems about small towns and big rivers, about streams and bars.

In the West, few writers then had audiences coast to coast. Actually, I think that the narratives were worn out: the same old stories of conquest and frontier. The land belonged to indigenous people.

We started Richard Hugo House fourteen years after Hugo had died. It became a "triggering town." That's what Hugo called small towns, real and imagined, that he used to "trigger" and inspire poems. Many of his finest poems are about towns way past their prime. So was our old Victorian, the structure where we set up housekeeping.

Writers, poets, playwrights, musicians, and artists came and performed. Nobel Laureate Seamus Heaney and poets Nikky Finney, James Tate, Donald Hall, and Lucille Clifton all read there. So did Chris Abani (also playing the saxophone), Jonathan Lethem, James Welch, Louise Erdrich, Gretel Ehrlich, Bill Kittredge, and Sharon Olds. The Black Cat Orchestra was our soundtrack.

Writers, and especially poets, just like Richard Hugo, love places on their way to becoming ruins. That's what this house was, a dusty example of failing Victorian splendor. Writers felt comfortable here, like they could try out anything. I mean you could spill stuff and no one would care. Physically spill. Emotionally spill. Whatever.

That's why, almost twenty years after it became Hugo House, when the building was slated to be torn down, it rattled us.

Demolition is a sad prospect. You could scream *Gentrification*. People do. I understand. But think past the sentimental, and imagine actually preserving the old place. Can you see it diminished next to the huge new buildings surrounding it? A spite house kept in defiance to the skyline?

I want to keep track of one thing. I want to press a thumbprint into a patch of dirt and say, *Remember what was here.* What happened with this land and the writers coming through, the crossroads of the place—I want to press it to something.

Don't we want to know that another city sung underneath this one? Or a village or crossing-over place? When such settlements are gone, what are we left with?

Some people say there were ghosts in the old house: sightings of a dead girl in the basement, the smell of burnt toast in the stairway, and the inexplicable floods through the ceilings on the night of my last reading there. That was the night the building really started to come down, even before the bulldozers arrived and headed off, beeping towards the clapboards.

Until now, I'd attached all those memories to this patch of land. Next, I'm trying to move that process into verse, into the ways that one poet follows another. Not in a historical postcard kind of way, not through black-and-white portraits that people can't focus into anymore. In some other way.

Gary died. It happened after we moved out. We had his funeral reception in the café, the same one that we lived above. When I think of him, I think of him mostly in Richard Hugo House.

My story is only one story. We remember places where we've lived, where we've moved from and then the places are torn away. I guess we make art in the face of loss— out of those little fissures and erasures in our lives. With luck, we see some overlaps, some things coming into view, and we push things together until they make sense. That's what poets do—only not exactly.

Timber Curtain. (*n.*) 1. The name given to a line of trees left after a logging sweep. *Origins:* Pacific Northwest, mid- to late twentieth century. Strung along the long roads of the Olympic Peninsula, the lines of trees were left to block sightlines of the clear-cuts. 2. *Urban version:* "façademies" (rhyming with lobotomies), the use of façades of old buildings as a decorative "curtain" for new, less ornate and often cheaply-made structures. *See also:* **Façadism.**

Unspooled, my roll of paper will cover the whole city. I'll staple one end to the lake's edge, along the madrones. Then, the sheet will spread across downtown, bunching at the hills, stretching all the way to the harbor. The sound is ferocious: a paper-made storm. I'll write on the overlay, marking clouds as the building cranes rip through.

Land, as you know, doesn't change. Not down deep. So, off we go—to the headwaters, to the source, upstream— with our bandanas on sticks. We shoulder ahead until we see the flush of grasses, the sill, brush, berry, and stone. Our boots to clay remind us: haunting is only paper deep. Most things disintegrate.

And so, we begin.

I.

ALONG WITH THE DEAD POET
RICHARD HUGO

Richard Hugo never lived here.
I lived here.
Hugo was a poet and I am a poet
but we didn't overlap.
At least not in life.
Or in this house. Not exactly.

This is Seattle.
A place to love whatever's left,
where new things are coming
shinier than the last. I'm the bust
standing in the boom,
the poet in the technology world
spread along the timber bottom.

Hugo wrote poems about places
nearby, ones you might overlook:
old spots on the river, rooming houses
by the freeway,
taverns of men "fresh from orphan wars."
He'd point you to some
part of the city
laid out by drunken pioneers and

tell you that maybe your life was already
coming apart:
just then, slack tides would surge
in your ears and the pallets
soaked in fish rot and wood
grew soft, clear runoff.

You'd lost things.
That's where you'd start.

GENTRIFICATION WEDGE

To us this part of the hill
felt like the suburbs
these cheap apartments
and warehouse blocks
just off downtown
the dark corridors
we found our ways into
the building once
a mortuary where people
said rosaries over caskets
in the chapel and open
wakes took place in the living
room where college kids took
calls to pick up bodies
and it was all we could
think about later
when the place was a theater
that smelled like beer
it was an ashtray
it was perfect
so we came into beer and ashes
and believed in the stage
where we put poets
and tellers of tales
we'd all need to hear
while the city whispered on
planning to suffocate
one thing after another
when you are young
you find what's overlooked
and you build there

CALL IT AN INTEREST

The disruption of disintegrating things—
any place on its way to becoming
a ruin.

Imagine driving up to the face
of sentimentality
and waving.

CRANES ON THE SKYLINE, COMING TOWARD US

Keeping track of
Just one
Place not so
Museum-worthy
But enough old
Stuff to make
Us ache for
Sightlines amidst
The plastic chutes
Where traffic lilts
Along in a stream
Not a new river
Or submerged creek
But alignment
The future begged
Sloppy intention
And its residue
What's not to stop
The riddle between
Us and what fills
It being downright
              [   ].

RETRACING MY STEPS

In our city, there's all this
replace, replace. Redo this,
remodel that. A game of pick up
and put away. Shell. Coin. Peanut.
Plastic housing slipped inside
old brick. I can't walk to the store
without missing bits.
Marks, treads and dust
shake out and underfoot what's left
disappears at the thresholds. Whish.

Let's reenact, replace,
repurpose our old ways.
Let's re, re, re all the way
to the re-tirement home,
let's tire ourselves again
and again. Re-place this
place and that place,
this once-salty patch
of earth smothered under
peat or stone,
brushed by salmon bones.

A teardown lets you let things go.
But, scrap gives back.
Tinkers come and poke.
Developers call it a footprint.
You pass along with your boots on:
a crime scene outline. Your life
aching in the *Gone*, shimmering.

BACK TO THE ORIGINS

Old smelters
crank out poems,
tapping into some river
of how things began,
how time and ambition
take the center and slash away
what could never have lasted while
these days, artists and musicians
move south, way south,
like Portland and Olympia
south. How the *forces of righteousness,*
rip down anything you could possibly love,
Richard Hugo wrote. Mills close; towns die
and that's a progression in the West:
earth belly up and sutured,
rivers rerouted by blue tarps twisted
past arsenic and lead sludge
no one can afford to clean up.
Make it new is a structural
problem, a capitalist problem
and the outsider's voice is any poet's
grumble at the switch—
mill-bound and let down, an homage.

TO CONJURE THE PAST IS TO BEG THE FUTURE FOR MORE

What was once bardic splendor, the lonely
rot where our walls quivered and lore spoke on,
one long nostalgic cry let out and then:
nothing. Give us the promise of a din,
the wheeze of carpet and old gin—where rooms
took shape as the poets paced their woozy
ruts, walked their wares between stage and lobby.
Read this, one would shout as the rest lined up.
What's the past but nostalgia's unwilling
bride, the clipped march of one still practicing
for the big day? Traditions kept up the way
tomorrow's rundown places take hold
while a chosen few clamber for the new
as they point to old ways blocking their view.

THE MIST TAKES HOLD

Places washed out in rain, towns gone past
and the Duwamish, a polluted old river,
flowing north to the mouth, along
brackish water in flats where Boeing
dumped acid for decades—
people in White Center are still
trying to get by. All these years.
Out by Mount Rainier
the Kapowsin Tavern burnt
to char and nails—embers in the wet—
and mist rolls soot into the mossy air.

In the aftermath, so long after,
we'll watch this old place come apart
while the destroyed water moves
up and out,
turning rubbish to salt.
Front row seats to the ruin,
our faces set, our limbs folded.
Have you ever seen such hope?

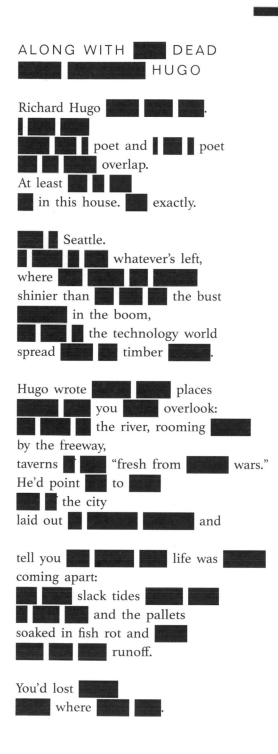

ALONG WITH ■ DEAD
■ ■ HUGO

Richard Hugo ■ ■ ■.
■ ■
■ ■ poet and ■ ■ poet
■ ■ overlap.
At least ■ ■ ■
■ in this house. ■ exactly.

■ ■ Seattle.
■ ■ ■ ■ whatever's left,
where ■ ■ ■ ■
shinier than ■ ■ ■ the bust
■ in the boom,
■ ■ ■ the technology world
spread ■ ■ timber ■.

Hugo wrote ■ ■ places
■ ■ you ■ overlook:
■ ■ ■ the river, rooming ■
by the freeway,
taverns ■ ■ "fresh from ■ wars."
He'd point ■ to ■
■ ■ the city
laid out ■ ■ ■ and

tell you ■ ■ ■ life was ■
coming apart:
■ ■ slack tides ■ ■
■ ■ ■ and the pallets
soaked in fish rot and ■
■ ■ ■ runoff.

You'd lost ■
■ where ■ ■.

To us this ▮ ▮ ▮ hill
felt ▮ ▮ ▮
▮ cheap ▮
and warehouse blocks
just off ▮
▮ dark corridors
we found our way ▮
▮ ▮ once
a mortuary where ▮
▮ ▮ ▮ ▮
▮ ▮ ▮ ▮ open
wakes took place in the living
▮ ▮ ▮ ▮
▮ to pick up bodies
and it was all ▮ ▮
▮ about ▮ ▮
▮ ▮ ▮ ▮ theater
that smelled ▮ ▮
▮ ▮ ▮ ▮
▮ ▮ perfect
so we came in ▮ ▮ ▮
and believed in ▮ ▮
▮ ▮ ▮ poets
and tellers ▮ ▮
▮ ▮ ▮ to hear
▮ the city whisper ▮ ▮
planning to suffocate
▮ ▮ ▮
▮ ▮ ▮ young
you ▮ ▮ overlooked
and ▮ ▮ there

II.

WHAT HAPPENED THERE

Rehearsals
Forty years before the house
became a theater, before those
actors and musicians showed up,
the Mannings had a mortuary
because a lot of Catholics needed
one. It was the 1930s.
The sons removed the old apartments
and put in viewing chambers,
embalming sinks, and later,
they added a big chapel.
People said rosaries. Priests themselves
were laid out: early examples
of product placement.
College boys lived upstairs
and took the calls for *Incoming*.
They played poker and climbed into
caskets. "Practice," one said.
Trouble then, when the satin ripped
and the lid slammed closed.

Second-Story Porch
George Plimpton with scotch, standing
at that railing upstairs. He looked out
and waved his glass. Across the street,
some guys were trying to get
the payphone to work. "Heroin connection,"
I said. One guy banged the box with
the receiver. "Fucking lousy shitface," he screamed.
Mr. Plimpton sipped. Then he looked at me.
He'd played a lot of roles in his writing—
baseball player, boxer, circus performer—
but he hadn't done this one yet.

In Our Apartment

Sherman Alexie wants to make a movie.
He asks to paint our bathroom.
Tomato red, it turns out.
Maddy has parties and kids
are swimming in that tub.
The walls are still red later,
when the house comes down.

The Baseball

With the crack came splintering,
then bristle-crunch and *thunk*.
A weird gasp of air caught us,
when the baseball took a hop
on my table and sunk to the floor.
A feathery hole
bloomed in the window.

We startled. Our quiet slipped;
my little girl stood up, holding the ball—
showing me. "Oh," she said.
Our work interrupted, her drawings
unfinished: lions mid-roar
and forests not grown, and mine—
mid-lyric, rhyme caught in air—
we looked at the ball.

We went outside to meet the boy
who slugged the thing
from the other end of the playfield.
"Home run," I said.
"Big hit," my daughter said.
We shook his hand.
We were all unharmed.

Breakfast

When Seamus Heaney showed,
we made him breakfast at the house.
Maddy clung to his knees and said, "Big voice."
Indeed. She was maybe three. Then he spoke and
gave toasts to the house, *May it bring writers
from all over and host them well:*
"To welcome a bewildered homing daughter
Before she even knocks," he'd written.
"What's this? What's this?" sang the poem,
"and they sit down in the shining room together..."

BELIEVE WHAT YOU WILL

1.

You don't have to believe in ghosts to accept
that the place was haunted. You know how
you shouldn't get crosswise with a magician?
Or how you shouldn't pull the lever
on a runaway trolley or even give in
to the *problem* of the trolley? Anything
caused by the downhill slide on rails—
or a ghost you don't believe in—is better left
alone. Who can say what an emergency
really is?
       Let's say a dead poet
roams the place. Not to be confused with
the actual dead girl who really does seem
gauzy and almost visible, even in the basement,
but this guy, the poet, wanders mostly upstairs.
Some say he's everywhere. Hyperbole,
that's his currency and his hauntings smell
like a trip through the toaster, a charred whiff.
Our aftermath began when we named the place
after him and hoped he'd linger there.
He overstayed and burrowed in.
Not like he poked a fishing pole in anyone's
eye or anything. Not as though the poet
himself were moaning or that he belches beer
and leaves muddy spots on the carpet.
Nor does he pace at night. It's his verse
that does that.
But Haunting is haunting.

2.

The girl appeared in the basement and floated
in and out of the air-well to the sky.
In those days, people used the yellow pages.
Maybe no one flipped through to get
hazy ghost girls out of their houses, but I did.
You might guess that a person doesn't
find *exorcism* or *spiritual cleansing* in directories
heaved onto your porch. You'll look under
some other heading and end up with a guy
wearing a tool belt, a man pointing
to the airshaft where the dead pigeons
stacked up. *Shoulda brought a pitchfork.*
Later, when he comes upstairs, job half done,
saying he'd "seen something," he didn't say
the word *ghosts* and who would? But
Haunted, as I said, is haunted. That's one part.
Then, the priest and wiccan and rabbi,
and Native healer—you can't be
too careful when it comes to presences—
they wave rods and beads and sage sticks,
even rosaries in what's to say a *dousing*.
The priest says *churning* as in *Spirits churning*.
You know when you pour a drain de-clogger
into the sink hole? And maybe you overdo
it and keep pouring, more than you need,
down and down, as if spiritual cleansing
could be real and the pigeons,
dead no more, could rise up and fly from the bin
and the man with the tool belt and his plans
go on as the birds wing away.
What if you do take twenty kids with
the healer and the rabbi and the wiccan
(who far outlasts the priest) nodding over

rods and murmuring as his arms twitched?
The little copper rods spin in the wiccan's hands.
Like fishing. Like the dead poet with his
bait hung over some riffle in the river.
Hit the line, he'd say. The wiccan chants,
Girl. A young girl over in the corner.
Where the river should have been, the poet sings.
Secrets really aren't. You don't have
to believe in them. Think of secrets as
containers with a short lease. Lines of poems
can be as serrated as land. The poet's were.
He wrote into our ears with the tin
that clinks in mills overturned by rivers
and the plink in your ears, even now:
Those sounds are hauntings. Our hauntings.

SIGHTLINES

People live in the park
across the street. Always did.
"Mr. Mayor," the assistant said,
"we design for sightlines."
To see from every angle, to gloat
from every bench and install barbs
on the rails so people will not
rest their heads, and we can
see inside whatever shelter there is.
That's what he meant.
Sightlines—the visibility of
our neighbors who try to live in the park.
More come. And there's no answer.
No policy that can save us.
In the meantime, the mayor's man says,
"We will be able to see everyone
who relieves himself here."
Then, he points to the bathrooms.

FOR WHAT IT WAS

When my daughter
Maddy said,
"Look, it's so shiny,"
and she pulled
the crack pipe
from the sand,
she looked so happy.
She held it up
and for a minute,
I let her hold it.
Then I took it away.
We lived where
we should have.
We didn't aspire
to more.
Rain pooled
in the swings;
syringes sang in the dirt.

ONE ARTIST'S BEGINNINGS

She smeared our windows with Vaseline.
Little fish, swimming upstream
out of her bed, into the halls.
Window by window she moved,
padding along with her jar,

smudging the panes.
She sang little hymns:
the sweet timbre of making things
as she toddled in her boots,
stood on chairs and wiped over
the rectangles and squares.

Beyond the apartment's
red door, in the cafe below,
poets slammed and drag queens
spun, words tippled, prose flew,
books slapped open
and closed, registers trilled,
whiskey poured, gyres collapsed,
people clapped and the laughs
whistled through the seams.

Where she worked: a little apartment
upstairs. Portals to clouds, the open lid
of a jewelry box pitched
sideways, our windows
were bleary glass cube
views of the city. Her tiny finger
drew figures
in the goo. Other fish, and her parents,
if they squinted,
could almost see through.

Her father found her,
our tiny trout girl,
asleep on the floor
while a delicious
calming light floated
our apartment up, up:
our glowing ship,
tipped on the hill.

In her room, our little chum
had passed by easels and crayons,
humming over paints and markers
and the wide canvas of the walls,
heading for new seas.
Into the lit aquarium, she'd swum.

IN THE WHISPER GONE,
YOU ARE A LITTLE GIRL

Summer wasn't that hot, back then. We never needed
air conditioners.

When we leaned out of the windows. When we were
spoons over the sills. Three of us.

The flap of a loose shake on the roof. Flap-itty, clack.
Lost gulls circling for the sound. The screeching
outside.

Foghorns, train whistles and the up-close clanking of
the ferries chaining up, cars coming off.

The sea smell rolled up the hill.

Chairs and tables. Old floor. The baby, you, stumbling.
Flutter of shadows, watery in the hallways. The
meandering.

And things put on ledges. The corner of the clothes dryer
in the basement. Diaper loads. Stack of animals,
stuffed, along your floor.

More cigarettes than now. Outside the apartment,
down on the street, people smoked there.

When your father was alive, it was grit and grunge
and rain.

And heroin. The payphone across the street where the
dealers called in. Packet to palm at the sidewalk spot.

Wet cedar in sniffs, greens along the bark. Reddening.
Rhododendron, waxy, coming around to bloom again.
Water in the sod, pooling.

Further back, the mill whined and choked through
timber. It was so soggy in historic times. Sawdust
smeared on the lot. Long before we came.

Sunlight through the slipknot gray. And green in it.
The rain was mist. Mulch and moss and water clear,
floating the needles.

Or urine whiffs tucked behind the fish gusts, briny
overture and dropped into the boot-suck at the curb.

From upstairs, the rush of applause through the floors,
the roar of flooding through the ceiling, later. Tearing
away what we loved. Ghosts through it.

What the hell is that noise?

Pigeon tomb in the air-well. Bird breasts filling up.
The stench and clog.

Your dad scraped the place out. Stuffed then emptied,
feather-full and feces. Then it clogged and filled with
water after he was gone. It kept on.

The locked gates weren't for the raccoons. They were
for people. We didn't tell you that.

What did we really need? Tables and those black
chairs with rips in the vinyl. Pulled around to see.

Careful, on the steps, not to fall. We said that
sometimes. You were unsteady in your boots.

Not so long ago! Not so.

When we were all alive. Each of us, then. A blowhole
on the edge of the horizon we did not see. Opening
and coming for us.

What brought us near matters of our spin. How we
could not see exactly, not in the sway.

You were such a little thing, the bottom margin of the
growth charts where we pushed a pin.

Cried if we lifted you back into the apartment.

You listened for the ghost girl. Put out a finger, not
pointing exactly, but feeling the wilt of air.

It was there. Just there,
it was.

III.

SAY YOU COME HERE

The city is yours, dim and rain-draped—
a metropolis where what could happen
falls finally upon you and so, on a whiff
of mist, you are following gusts
pinched through the streets,
along pavement silted, spit-spat.
See that blocked-off lot?
Two huge cedars along the fence.
Peruse through broken slats:
a borrow pit, where the house was.

WHY REAL ESTATE IS SO EMOTIONAL

We'd lived upstage in the theater, beyond
the curtains, past the prop rooms.
There, we left our shoes; we carted our bags;
we cooked our eggs, put on our trousers.
Fed the baby, warmed her bottles,
watched as she rolled little trams
to the station under the bed.
We tumbled gym shoes
and cowboy boots in the hall,
left our jackets over the backs of chairs,
toppled stacks of books.
Sang to Sid Vicious and made heaps
of Rice-A-Roni. Up and down, car seat,
bibs and diapers affixed.
We groused, we fidgeted,
we spun along to The Kinks.
Sweet wonder of domestics.

To conflate the place
with our states of being—
a simple mistake, a turn undone
even when we'd migrated on
we longed for what resonated—
the curtain that shaped our stage,
collapsed in the corner.
Everything came to an end:
the house with writers and actors,
with musicians rushing about.
The chapel-theater, the stands.
Lives flipped with performances,
with curtains opening and opening.
The look-back a wave, then a nod,
then some small keepsake, a word.

IF YOU REALLY WANT
URBAN PLANNING

There should be a river here.
Let it run by the house that was,
the place that was, the land that is.
Past the water's could-be drift
and briny turn, a woman will be

pushing a dinghy overhead.
See how she sets off from the old
shacks to the new city? Through
loose trees along the hill, she'll
weave, sliding her skiff to the sea.

To mark her way is to reach up
and sketch turns on cloud paper
as planners do—one move
to another, pulling new streets
into view: *Just there* in a billowing

paper wish: she's lifting
her little boat to where,
where would be the shore.

IF YOU REALLY WANT

a river here.
by the house that was,

a woman will

weave

sketch turns on cloud paper
as planners do—
pulling
a billowing

paper wish:

THE MEASURE OF MY RETURNS

1.

At first, the ghosts were toast burners
and the dead girl, wispy in her returns,
wandering and whirling—holdovers
from the long-gone funeral home.
And then, the phantoms were my own.

When the building splintered down,
my dead fathers arrived. They found
their way to the rubble and thrummed
at the fence. My old home had begun
to disappear and we were left to face
our losses at the scraped-away place.

2.

One father has a cigarette
and a hole in his throat, whistling
Have you a match?
The other father is eating a doughnut
and pointing
to the hole in the ground,
*Should have found something
more permanent,* he suggests.
The first one sputters, *Time to move on.*
He tries to count backwards.

3.

My husband does not show.
Neither does Richard Hugo.
They weren't pulled into the wake
of loss for my sake—
both ghosting on, choosing to live
at a campsite along the ridge
or in the watery shadows
where trains passed, dark and slow.
While the fathers stand
at the lip of excavation, severed
man-kin who'd long followed me in.
I survived, I say to each,
feeling the flank of my own speech
leaning against me and seizing relief.

TRYING TO GET BY

A person can imitate being.
Putting on shoes.
Opening doors. Pull.
Taking a seat in the office.
Quiet. She can stay alive until
spheres of consciousness
overlap and focus. On say,
a telescope. A neighbor's window
or that book, creased open.
When a body is left out,
ready for claiming and discarding,
how much intention
could there be? *Corpse,
cadaver,* it's lost on me.
I'm fumbling now, toward it,
weak with how much
once went on—then
the sudden calm.
I can live alone.
It's one more
country to be in.
Another region where
pain fills my lungs
and pushes me to
swim around an island,
one that grows bigger
while I grow more and more fit
to be immersed,
spinning around and around it.

FIXING IN PLACE

If I could fold our findings into the mouths
of the dead.
If I could plant these souvenirs into
a poet's tomb,
into my husband's plot. If I could tuck
what I know beneath
all things taken down. If I could go back
and fix one thing.
If I could find the country where more is
less the norm.
If I could take the memory stick and wish
it to a willow switch,
if I could swat the longing right out of us.
Steles, corpuscles, root
matter and the clatter of people. If I could
walk betwcen clouds.
The little girl who lived here, twenty now,
who once laughed
and trotted across the floors,
up to the stage. If I
could listen now as she sang when she
was not supposed to.
If her father would come back and if we
could wave her on.
Again. If I could keep waving. If he could. If We.

MAYBE THIS BUILDING SHOULD GO

What else to do when something is
dying? You say, finally, *let it.*

This city block, now slated for
teardown—it's not your childhood,

not you, that building.
Every sentimentalist for miles says:

My heart is in that place and *no,
don't make another thing*

*go away. Don't erase and replace
places we didn't know we loved.*

It's just this: an old Victorian
with a plywood cube nailed on.

As the white sign goes up,
we see what's to come down

in city-speak. Soon enough someone
tags the sign. Indigenous-like.

Marks that might be Salish for
Don't take one more thing away.

It's not memory that lasts,
but the terrain. Old land: claimed

and staked and stolen. Old.
Conquest taunts the bulldozer,

nose up, claws grasping, heading into it.

What else to do when something is
dying? You say, finally, *let it.*

        your childhood,

with a plywood cube nailed on.

Marks that might be Salish for

                claimed

and staked and stolen.

THIS

stolen.

IV.

TAKE THE OLD DREAM

Driving the West is a way of seeing how
desolate home is, how warm
once you get there—
boots tipped to heels
at the hearth, or the mud and slag
by the step of the double-wide.
Our terrain out here is a way of saying
Get going or *Take this.*
Let's say that we homesteaded
and no greed was involved.
Conquest was papered over
and we took it as courage.
Claims of places to call
Home or *Mine* floated wide,
drifting out from the withered sides
of the two-lane highway.

As I stood in the ruins of an old mill
something came loose
inside of me: the years of places
I'd come from fading inside
that old foundry I didn't have
to rely on anymore. Rage
fell under the ore crusher,
and shifted en route to the smelter
while I drove full on,
one old town inside my ribs
and another just off the interstate
until I imagined my way clear;
love distended, the caesura of my waking
lifted cityless into the plains.

EVEN AS IT ROTS, YOU CAN'T MOVE IT

Crowds come to our part of the world.
Some stay. Others bend away
from the policemen's clubs, huddled
under the Occupy or homeless tents
within the steam of tear gas or fog seeping in.
Our city is a wreck shining on the hill.
Nothing gritty like that can stay:
not the stalwart-once
bulwark, the sagging,
mossy ship on the slope.
Cockeyed in memory it turns,
rotting from underneath:
the slow rotation and creaking
from timber to kindling—
burnt in the clear glass spleen
built to preserve everything.

OLD TALK ABOUT THE WEST

Remember the joke where the guy comes
        into a bar and then it's America?
He's in America. In that bar.
        Or the one where three guys come
to America and then they work until their bootstraps
        rip out and they become rich?
Remember that one? Punchlines never say this:
        You don't always get what you deserve.
The past makes everything smaller, more fragile,
        as if it were shot in a diorama.
Did you know that Bill Gates went east and came back?
        Or that the hippies are gone? Loggers too?
The fishermen are almost gone. The weather is
        warmer. Not so much rain.
Truly, homesteading is over. Unless you are
        buying an interest in vacation property.
The West is a good place to feel well—
        if you move away from Hanford.
Some people try to recuperate and feel worse
        except at the spa ranches.
People aren't finding themselves anymore.
        Finding a living is harder and
cities are not a last resort.
        They are resorts.
You won't put your life together here.
        It's as good a place as any to fall apart.
Something new is switch-backing towards us,
        guns blazing, barns raising, ranch spreading,
city herding, screens glowing, and everything exploding—
        newcomers cower in the confines of our myths.

MIGRATION HATRED

I.

We cried when our childhoods
left us, and later, when our places went—
old apartments Over-the-Rhine,
where Cincinnati's Germans settled
in some unlikely climb to status,
while my people, those Irish,
stared down the rent with everyone
else who landed: the Great Migration
folk and Appalachian hill people.
Long afterward, artists came; then
dot-com boomers arrived and digitized
Over-the-Rhine. They gentrified.

All routes led to migration
hatred: riots and blame tangled
in displacement: markers of where
someone's people lived and then
didn't. Take the Mason-Dixon Line,
the fissure of the river I climbed past
to go west. Back then, I'd thought
it was a border for Capture the Flag or
Red Rover, Red Rover
Send the Yankee Over.
The Ohio was a watery fence,
a gateway's flush to the south,
steamboats and cholera in
the same knocking spin
of the paddlewheel I'd hear
later when timber hit the docks.

II.

When I was ten, I was in someone's basement
where an older kid played
Bye, bye Miss American Pie
while upstairs, in the living room, some ladies
had a Daughters of the Confederacy
meeting. The future then was beneath them.
But they never knew how we children
plotted from below, how we'd see the levies go
dry and the good old boys run out of rye
as we became the newest colonists
who, step by step, would undomesticate
all that was stolen and handed to us.

GRATITUDE

For a while I thanked the wrong people.
I climbed up ladders and washed windows
for residents who wanted unmarred views.
"You should be grateful," said one from below.
"I bought a nice ladder for you to use."
"Oh I am," I said, climbing rung to rung
up to the roof muck. Then I reached over
the gutter ledges, into the eaves.

I imagined a windstorm coming out
of the forest and turning headlong to shore:
glass bending in the frames of the house;
grout turning sand and wood into more
dust, the reprise of a grateful universe
rebelling, and no one left to keep it clear.

NOT EXACTLY

The Jungle is an encampment
for homeless people in Seattle.

The Jungle was a refugee camp
in Calais, France.

The jungle is a place in Brazil
where wild animals live.

My pockets are full right now.
I'm on the fringe of acceptable speech.

The edge of confirming
someone's suspicions. Trust me,

I have a habitat and jungle
it isn't. And I live in a city,

a city in America where mayors
designate little huts to put scuffles

at bay, but guns go off.
People are suffering. The rest of us

with rooms, we shift our gaze to
the wild in the wild and say that

we can't bear the shots.
Or the children muffled in hunger.

A rope is as strong as an impulse:
it strains and grows longer.

Some ropes lead into the jungle
where they fray. How long since people's

homes were bulldozed anywhere,
not just in Calais? How long until

guitars slide and horns moan
under downpours everywhere,

scattering the newly landed, the long-
dismissed-from-dwellings, strewn

across broken cement—plunk, plunk—
and torn away? In our warm tunnels,

in our studios, we're stuffed as a wink
beneath the eaves and we try to live with

cleared and stripped jungles in the nearby
outdoors: gatherings in places without

beams and floors.

CONSOLATION

Mote-strewn, terrarium of little storms:
My room fills with metronomes.
I walk among them. On some afternoons,

I can barely hear the tut-tut between
thunder breaks or table saws
(the saw-loud glade of my days).

Backwards, the mechanisms trot
to the same swaddle-click, swaddle-click—
spindle flip in the box slots.

Inside my chest is the flutter and inside
my mind is the rain. And inside that:
a spitter-day when the river thrums along.

I'm in waders slipping on the stones,
humming click-trout, click-trout and fly-snap,
setting a clip to the reel. Casts are sizzles

laid flat. Upstream the ticky-frump of dusty
clocks lines the backstock of town shops.
To syncopate and keep the world in time,

hold the slant of water to the sea
or the storms that tock over the tables.
I'm at the threshold, in front of the hearth,

conducting my heart out, metronomes
just fine and my hands unfurling to clicks
of stream and strewn, looking out, into the room.

SOL   O

metronomes.

Inside my chest is the flutter and
              the rain.
a

                    ticky-frump of dusty
clocks

          slant
       storms that tock
    at the   hearth,

          and my   unfurling
             strewn,   into the room.

MONKEY IN TRAINING

The typewriter wrote the story with its own keys.
Meeting its end here in the pawn shop,
set atop a plate in the window, the machine
is awaiting one more go, with someone, anyone it seems.
Every story will come eventually.
Put a monkey at the letters and expect
to wait. The story inside the typewriter percolates.

When I was a child at school, my mother
arranged typing lessons with the secretary.
My mother said that I'd need a job. But I never
really understood what she meant.
Would I become the one to stage displays,
manning the tills of pawn shops or
doing what I always did: lying in wait
for someone to say something?

"No," my teacher said. "Follow the instructions.
No extra words." There, you see, was my training:
tracing the workbook drills with a typewriter
that didn't have the right inclinations.
Later, I saw the contraption upon its plate,
stilled from plunking stories
that weren't possible from me.
Wailing and punching my way
against instruction, I awoke.
Monkey girl at the ready, alert, coaxing
every tale I could from the orphans
around me, from one key to the next.
Rescuers, I learned, do not descend floating.
Instead, all the poets rise from their daguerreotypes,
whistling, standing by the curtain,
readying themselves for performance
no matter what stories await them on stage.

ART MONSTER

We made him in our neighborhood.
From spilled flour and sawdust,
with little bits glued on and tugged upright,
he turned into, well, a *someone*.
A someone-something
alchemized because our craving
for plot and plot and plot became
too much. Exhausting, actually.
The potential pace of "Go here and
here and here and then and then"
made us want to cry under the weight
of it. Or just lie down in the road.

So we made him into a plot-slower,
our Mosaic Creature—he was Art Monster,
almost the dictator's
orange-headed doppelganger.
Only less menacing. We tried
kitsch, beloved detritus—
and we built him from a wish,
a curdling intention to slow movement
and deflect current events a bit.

Night after night, one of us
snapped shut the pockets on his shirt.
We dusted him off and sent him
to galleries and receptions.
Poverty, brutality, ill health,
the terrible waters rising,
shrouds of gas and acids
that were killing everything—
Art Monster avoided this.
Instead, he developed simple theories.

73

People fussed over him.
Our glee was waning fast
as our plotless wonder, our grounded bird,
stumbled through his after-glory.
Each of us, the makers, became
sheepish in our desires. The placards
describing Mr. Monster's
work diminished.
We felt our way away from him.
Ready to console, our inhales choking,
"Art Monster," we begged, "Be beautiful
so we can love you."
His identity slipped his wrapping,
while our hometowns
finally, savagely, let us go.

THE STREET SONG LAST ON
EVERYONE'S LIPS

Of his suits! Of Baudelaire's
apparel, something must be said.
His hems dragged in the dirt;
his neck spoiled his collars and
in the midst of strolling,
florid in his pace, the poet
muttered snippets and
crisscrossed the blocks—
a 19th-century version of
our hipster-loner now
on walking sojourns
roaming in the reedy call
of night-ways through the city's
laid-out prose, the *flaneur.*
He sought hideouts. He hid
his findings in the boxes
of poems, the way metropolis
blocks tucked in the shops.

But Paris is one thing, Seattle another.
The grand boulevards in America's West
trail into tech domes and wired lobbies.
Meanwhile, in Berlin, pedestrians
are roaming dead munitions factories,
barracks or the abandoned airport
Hitler built. In the cities of America,
citizens step to curbs and greet
the corsets of their phones.
Seattle's new apartments are lifted in
to the lot-sockets down below.

Our flaneur is caught in the neoliberal
sweep of commerce and vast, invisible
machinery. Corporatewise, *Globalized*,
the center held all too well, it seemed.
Real estate: paper's intention
erased. Restaurants: the new
extraction economy. Meetings:
locations faced on the internet.
In the lands of screens rolling,
of controllers tipped, gamers
sit in darkened quarters. Our flaneur,
nouveau Baudelaire, is a collaborator
in spirit, longing to wander into the players'
chambers, and sit amidst potato chip
grit, alongside them on the couch. He'd whisper,
Please my dears. May I play at it? For a little bit?

TIMBER CURTAIN

1. Sound Check

On the stage, someone says,
One-two, test-ing you, one-two
and flicks the pop foam
atop the microphone.
Can you hear me?
Deeper, the voice booms.

*

Sea swells knock
a hundred miles off
at the Natives' shore:
tides thundering
with logs, roots affixed,
floating cedars
heaped upon the beach.
Behind them, tree-felling
thrums and seethes,
tombing the forest—

*

In the city, in front of the stage,
the chairs spin and the curtain
spool-thumps open.
Boots and tables knocking,
glasses tapping, the audience
taking root, looking on.
Then: Night talking begins
in the land of watchers.

2. All Sorts of Music Starting Up

Imagine that timber road to the sea—
think of driving down the corridor of fir and pine,
straight along a pavement stripe, and seeing
zips of light—streaking splits between trees:
flash-clip, flash-clip, metronomic flicks
and behind: the sky of the clear-cut.
Metal green. Logged clear.

Scotch broom and junk timber tangle
where sun fists through.
See how the trees soften your vision?
Moving as you do, in and out of the fog?

3. Two Places Can't Overlap Exactly

In this house, on that stage,
the poet is dismayed.
Nothing can convey the trees,
the feeling of savagery,
with this microphone,
under those lights.
The poet starts:

> *Apart is a way*
of being.
> *The way a part*
is ground
> *down as sunlight*
in the clear-cut
> *cut clear to morning.*

Try though a bard might,
Mourning, the poet thinks.
Ground, the poem says.

4. All Sorts of Tools

From the confines of the car
you can see through the curtain of trees
into that open, vacant place
where the mechanisms of loss
increase: Skidders, Feller-bunchers
plain old Ripper-outers.
Brush, a torn mass, coming in.
The ground blinking to the sun,
glimmering machinery.

5. The Practical Matter

Timber built the house.
Hearts of cedars, these beams
where hill ladies once looked out.
Water carved the views
and now a poet reads
from a timber peel
into the clear-cut, the dark
expanse beyond the stage.
Talkers in the night,
cradled in the crossing-over
darkness, take a city-mist
glimpse. To the hills, to the sea—
as if to hear the shovel
and scrape of the regrade
when lumber men cleared
the slopes, our poet reached a pitch
and stepped behind the curtain.

6. The Cost of It

Gyppo loggers lived in Forks,
and took out trees
from Hood Canal to the sea.

They tossed chainsaws into
trucks, and climbed
through slope and drain

to see what else was left.
A few trees behind
the curtain—green

needles in the mist—
and the road ahead:
swishing in the wet.

7. Finally, Here

X is where the poet stands,
our shore-weary bird,
vulture with the snapped beak,
slipping into words.
Such is the place where the logger
stood, a mirror stage far off—
the curtain pulled, the land
besotted—a poet performed
within the possible.

A frontier shrinks. The trees go.
To startle as an animal does
and groan as sky roars in.
Wood sliced through
a mill on the Duwamish.
Stage watchers look for
what's to come:
a poet's little ends, the bits.

8. A Song Will Help

The poet sings,

Timber, Timber,
Curtain, Curtain.

Where the river should have been,
Where everyone we loved returned.
Where we re-re-re-placed our ways,
Timber took us there.
Where the river should have been
Where the river should have been,
It erased us at the shore.

9. Prophesy

Here was the plight we'd come to—
the land becoming land again,
undertowed in the reeds,
beyond the picks and shovels.
From the theater, the watchers
imagined all of it. They could see
driftwood that lumber made,
the waving drapery of city and forest,
and how it all came down,
like velvet, like cedar.
The places finally did converge,
in the poet's footprints on the stage.

No one yells *Timber* anymore.
Curtain! shouted the stage manager.
And, while he spoke, he activated the remote.

TIMBER CURTAIN REDUX

Tree Tree Tree Tree Tree Tree Tree Tree Tree Tree

	The
X	clear-
(where	cut
you	and
stand)	the
	stage.

Curtain Curtain Curtain Curtain Curtain Curtain

HEART OF THE CEDAR

It never snows here anymore.
Rain grays the walks and tins

the sky where blue
would have been.

I'll step back and let
the shutter's twitch

digitize it. Make it vapor.
Make it vapor on the paper.

I heard my husband's voice
on a long-ago

recording: little fibers
and yarns that spun

through the tape.
Whatever made it,

whatever made it so,
after he'd gone,

I thought I could not love

his voice anymore.
Slippage is the first

lesson of censorship.
Memory bitten

out of fear takes more.
Snow came and filled in.

I came to the erased
as if I'd crossed

into a field and found
what fabrics hung

warm once when
I'd left there.

AT THE RIVER MOUTH

The dock—ship mulch in the stick bed,
And I'm knee-deep to the reeds.

Long-rot pilings blur under snowy mud
Dredged up at the tide's lip

And the boat, what's left of it,
Rests just out of reach. Even the shed

Tilts with wet and the sea-line
Trips against the net of trees.

Dark, the river carves between us,
Brackish in the flat slough.

Gulp-heaves of fire once blew
And smoldered here, confounding

Mist. Oh! The fire happened
Long ago? Well, fog reenacts

The burn and leaves hunger
Through the simple white shell

Of a tree. The core is here. I'm reaching
Across the stones. See me over here?

Where goes the land's curve
The heart will follow—down slant

From the mountain's ribs.
Tinder-lit and timber stripped

Of all the bark. Nothing fits. The river
Is sinking, wood clenched against

The wilds, all wet, never drying.

PRACTICAL

> *...the curtains of trees, the rows of houses, the*
> *streets, the riverbed itself, that angular stability*
> *which so well prepares the shapes of property, all*
> *that was erased, extended from angle to plane...*
> *thereby suspending human becoming, detaching it...*
>
> **ROLAND BARTHES,** "PARIS NOT FLOODED"

The boom now, later bust,
thrum of buildings stripped and redone—
all the trolley tos and froms.
Downtown's upside on the hill.
Everything tumbles under the crane.
Years.
Do the ghosts travel,
following the land,
or do they disappear
within husk and gravel?
Do they reside inside
the monument that follows?
In the afterwards
we are living as we lived when we
imagined the now of the take-down.
My once gone home. My finally fall in the way down place.

THE WIND UP

How would I find you? As you were before?
Or are you like the person I've become,
Far into the dark, and far from home?

HOWARD MOSS, "THE BUILDING"

The city erasing itself and the building
where I find you, if I could find you,

comes into focus, then out. I'm pointing
to the site where you worked, the once-was

place. In that gesture, I could still feel
local. If those years came back over us,

returned in lathe and plaster, with
the red door slipping on its hinges,

would you be there, tucked in that dingy
house with me? I could look up to where

we loved each other. Or down, to that spot
where the building fell. Years torqued

over us—like the splintered old stairway.
Would you be in the knockings, the little

settlings rumbling under our boards?
Some things are so simple. Like wanting

the past back for a re-do or a glimmer
of you as a new character within it.

When we bundled the box in a truck,
not much of you was left. Not much.

Just the *here* that was going away,
leaving the remains of this earth and

not the parts we'd known upon it.
Your remains were not exactly the body

you'd known, but what remained when
all you once knew and left behind

combined with how I told it.
That's the husk—what had been sung

and left. Where your body was.
Where I am less. Where I am lighter,

snapped back then flung into a world
of beloved, disappearing scrap.

U P

How
  are you like the
    dark, and far from home?
HOWARD MOSS, "THE BUILDING"

The city erasing
            you,

      into

                          the once-was

place.

                              where

we loved each other
                  fell Years

settling

not much of you   left.

the husk—

Where your body was.
Where I am

          flung into a world
beloved, disappearing

V.

IF ICEBERGS WERE SHIPS

it would be the beginning of a lot of things.
Endings are that way.
We'd rather have the shell than the craft
made new. A lawn chair's view.
What is there that loves a demolition?
See the door? That earthquake-ready
threshold that we once stood in?
Door is an idea that hovers,
a slip of earth where we map
some other entrance.
One I am going to. One laid out for each of us
to lift ourselves though.

CEDAR THEATER

Through the curtain of trees,
we traveled to the stage.
The land was cut to clear
along the angles bladed

while the plight of rain
dipped the slope askew.
We came into the terrain
of the timber room.

A lidless place, but for fog.
Miles out, the squalling
sea froth smudged on bights:
a red boat tipping in the trawl.

The forest, upended there,
was a lumber-scree
unleashed, a run of snared,
disheveled ghost trees:

roots cut from the upper
growth braided in the gnarl,
while the wind's brush shuddered
through the dirt and snarl.

The way a lumberman
might wrap his coat and sniff
the air, we took the span
and held it in; the whiff

of bark once spat by saws
now lifted off into trucks.
We turned and left, but paused
for all the timber shucked

and tossed to freight. Our other
clear-cut formed a stage,
one planked and covered
indoors: a theater made

from timber in the core
of our city. We lined
the stage and unfurled
a curtain, the plot unmined

until the verse took hold
when the poets came,
stepping into folds
of the velvets, timber-tamed.

THE FRONTIER ROOM

Neon, blinking a bit, the sign
bolted to the brick in the unlit
part of downtown. An ode
to logging, a timber smoke
ballad turned to punk aches
of heroin-saturated faces
when kids came in, wet boots
through the sawdust, gin up
at the barstools.

The flickers pulled us inside,
and the noise. When guitars
slashed, when they cut so
music filled the dank,
when the drums slapped
and sticks cracked, when
kids shot up and spilled out
by the drag shows
at the Won-Ton Restaurant
or turned up by the lake,
we forgot the sour parts.

I never could see through
delight to a problem, not before
we slam-danced it to death,
screaming for nostalgia, right up
to after it became an end.

                              pain
             songs
                   steering
                   along the lake

   a rifle to   your sweet   head
                                        No   *gun*
                                        yesterdays
        As the   twang shriek
             flipped back
                        past the beach
             you are   smeared

Into the Seattle we've sleekly become

                        Nevermind
                        the world   so damaged

                              and cheap
        To a boy who slept

                against the big cedar
                                        finally fallen away

                where kids

Tossed here
                                   and you too

Lumber-numbed

With everyone

Knowing

                              the sway

        riff and slouch
                        with so much
        to   repair   and   console
        We were singing   *No I don't have a gun*
Holding our books up to our ears listening for clues
        Boys knitted and girls twirled their hair and we rattled through
Poems until they told us something—the big tarot of being alive

        Boy by boy the world
                              glimmered in the mist

                              becoming little ghosts
        Our city shifting   our planked-up taverns
And   low-grade melancholy

                        came down   on and on
        Blond and blood   music
        broken

WHERE DID YOU GO, KURT COBAIN?

Here's a more-than-twenty-years-later scream for you boy-man
    Clorox-haired singer and the pain
Amidst riches that songs could not cure
    I'm banging the steering wheel in my sing-along way
While my screech heaves along the lake
    Just down this boulevard just down here
You put a rifle to your chin to your sweet blond head
    And I was shouting *I don't have a gun No I don't have a gun*
Whammy across the water taunting like all yesterdays
    As the cap-splat of the shot and the twang shriek
Of the song flipped back for years and I hear it
    When I drive past the beach and can't help singing
Even now as you are the boy in long johns and smeared
    T-shirts and me backstage where the scream still leaks
Into the Seattle we've sleekly become
    All that glass and wood scrubbed free of moss

I was a teacher young then and my high schoolers lit
    Candles and put up *Nevermind* posters and *Bleach* handbills
Wanting to know how could the world be so damaged
    Even when you were rich and these kids were sort of rich
A lot of them really so like a quick and cheap heroin fix
    To a boy who slept on top of the radiator in class
I pass your old house Nirvana boy where a set of golf clubs
    Rests against the big cedar gate and grown-ups live there now
All the astrologers and dealers and hangers-on finally fallen away
    Next to the park with scorches in the bench, candle wax
Frozen on the planks where kids sit as little protopunks
    Showing up from Omaha or Asheville or Cheyenne
Tossed here like you from a dead town like Aberdeen
    I could have been one of them and you too
Lumber-numbed and netted from a storm waiting to reappear

With everyone else I went to Seattle Center for the memorial
When Courtney Love screamed a suicide note over the speakers
       And we prayed no kids would copycat your gun to chin
Knowing that the bands back then opened a backstage where kids lived,
       Where they plucked and shrieked and fell in as kin
All the heroin they could shoot or hoof in the sway of being alive
       Together without real talk just the old anthropology
Of riff and slouch maybe making out at The Crocodile
       And my classes with so much British Lit so much bland
I wanted to have art repair things and music console even while
       We were singing *And I don't have a gun No I don't have a gun*
Holding our books up to our ears listening for clues
       Boys knitted and girls twirled their hair and we rattled through
Poems until they told us something—the big tarot of being alive

       Boy by boy the world came into our city and the moss
Slid from the old roofs and windows glimmered in the mist
       Long flannels and lumber plaids that became fashion
Writers grew into prophets with day jobs
       At night one of us swept the private school hallways
Along the Olmstead greenway where you lived
       Kurt the boy from Aberdeen never in a classroom where
Azaleas bloomed outside and books lay on the table
       Once you lived under a bridge rotted with barnacle
Stink and pulp but *he likes to sing along he likes to shoot his gun*
       But he don't know what it means
I was on my scooter past your house and it was all
       Police cars and crime tape and people and I had to go
Miles over the hill over Jackson Street where Ray Charles
       Used to play back to the school and the lawn filled with kids
Who were smoking and becoming little ghosts of themselves
       Our city shifting too our planked-up taverns
And beery docks and low-grade melancholy
       Giving in to the plink plunk of cellos and guitars all shiny
While the old pool halls came down and knowing it would go on and on
       Blond and blood taken in, all the music pushed aside
Along the broken turns of Lake Washington Boulevard.

GOOD INTENTIONS

Not to prickle the ghost
Or trample the lambs,
Not to unravel the spin
Of swans, the herons
Who land, not to pull
The buoys that keel
Or wade into riffs
That the waves slip
Upon shore—
But to sing
Amidst the roar.

I am not graceful,
But I have flown.
In some lands
A glass of water could
Become a rose.
It takes a long time,
But it does happen.
What to do now, each day,
When waking upon swords?

A WORD ABOUT NOSTALGIA

How quickly the past shines—
pawn shops and brothels, moose antler velvets
pinned in the tavern.

Our longing redacts the violence:
memory, the harshest art
of censorship.

ANOTHER WAY TO SEE IT

Memories, stories—they linger.
I am outside the building now,
standing on the porch.
You can point to the stairs, how they
sighed just near the bottom,
hollow to the foot thumps.
But memories turn historical.
Shanks of cold case bits,
old coats mildewed and frozen.
Sleeves and buttons—remember
how you could try them on?

IF ONCE MY CITIES MERGED

What you await is just now being born.
The one you're seeking will begin to sing.

ADAM ZAGAJEWSKI, "DECEMBER"

Our city, gray and slow, hadn't the long sag
of dictatorship, though our colonizers took
Duwamish land and stripped it into real estate.
We had no castles just the strum and dram
of flim-flam wooden structures whisked off
in demolition trucks. One more café. That one
where we sat and took in the city: a steely,
shimmering afterglow. If I were aflame

with the rage of it, I would take to the gates
and wait for every man in a yellow vest
to arrive and depart. I'd know the way then,
the way change zinged into our land and
scrapped our sightlines. My days in the house,
so clear and sharp, are caught in mustard light—
I would not forget what lingered.

So I took to pinning things on the ceiling dome.
Blotting clouds aloft, imagining the what's-to-come,
I pointed to our volcanos, our earthquakes
and the now: a distant rocking of wars.
We hear them. In the canopies of our trees.
We are buried beneath the living.
We were one people at one part of a century.

CROSSING OVER THE
CROSSING-OVER LAND

AFTER FATIMA MERNISSI

A woman is a nomad when she crosses over
water. When she trails away from the rutted
folds in the farm-ground, when she points home
and says, *I've known it*, and takes her path
away. To take the route over rivers, to pass
above oceans, to put her foot upon the bridges,
to rest her head in foreign beds and awaken to birds
she hadn't heard. The goings-on and the left-
behinds, waving at the fences.

Remember how the baby wanted this or that?
Or when she was tired and wanted nothing?
A little thing trying to spin
up the growth charts?
How things were, and then
they weren't. Looking into
the mighty chamber of hindsight,
all expectation for the undoing
of the already done. To gape at it!
To mistake a house for the lives
inside and then to furrow out.
One apartment is a placemat,
the table reduced to chores.
Her travel offers settings for one,
with little left for more.
And then she was alone:
the whisper of one child,
grown. And she, tipping up
and slipping into the flown.

OLD WORLD RECOVERY

Where not the buyer came, we sold the stove anyway
to the neighbor and made kindling on the concrete.
Gone the tuber crop and our nutrition waned
until we blamed no greens and a lack of protein
for our minds' failings. Sleep did not help.
If we'd taken to the bed for longer, we'd have less
than we have now. The house emptied except
for the charcoal and kettle, the kindling and flame,
where we blanched our nestlings and boiled for tea,
smudged silt along our arms, sipped and pronged
our takings, our leavings. We took in the view.
Days turned and old ideas took liens against us
until we were our old selves, reset in place.
Blessed, socket by socket, we moved again.

LIVING WITH EMERGENCIES

Just before the end, the pilot is saying
Something Official from the cockpit,
and the squawks of fuzz and chatter
rewind in a black box dream of late-stage
urgencies and controlling orbits
that fail, zigging planes held midair just after
straight flight. Imagine the wing
of the machine jutting as a fin from the sea.

Rescuers stack up wreckage
caught in a toxic sludge of hope,
and the black lockbox can't be mapped.
Not without sorcery and persistence,
or a blinking bit that catches wind.

An eighty-year-old friend comes to stay
and she says that she is her own
black box, a copy-over tape of what she'd
stored before. Across the withers, I'm
twitching with injection wishes and then
I point to it: This part survived,
this half-mast grief that seeks residence
in my ribs and then doesn't.
The long turn comes, she said.
We all go, one by one,
bobbing in the near sea,
stranded on the far parchment.

THE PANIC MERCHANT

I'm fully clothed and shaking
on a warm day with the heat
blasting from the bathroom vent.

I can't get warm. I can't get dry.
Moss drips and the cedars form
brooms that sweep as the winds

push and water lifts. The world
passes me, gently, and it's given
me some things, like being young

for a while. The beach, raggedy
on the sound, was once a wafer's
edge. The trail I'd often climbed

slid down and a pier replaces
it now. Enough longing
and something slips historic.

Sorrow lets you live anywhere.
I know that grief is love's
turn and still I traded in

worry; I fretted with longing.
I future-tripped and ghost-
waddled, living ahead

of my living. Wind is ancient
through cedars. What could I not
love in the face of it? Pretend

I am carrying a bundle of sticks.
All the left-behinds carry sticks:
women on the donkey paths,

bearing up under the mountain's
slant, the heat. Our heritage is
made every day we are not

dead at war. People come and
take up camp. *Residence*
isn't *sanctuary*. Not anymore.

THE

day

warm.

Enough longing

lets
grief
turn

and

take up
sanctuary.

FLATTENING MORTAR

The city blooms umbrellas.
Salt rubs the edges of the building.
My glove, tapped against my cheek, is
an animal's muzzle, a wish
for relief. For the touch of things
being set right. My daughter is grown up
and I could write a widow's handbook
or a guide to living in buildings gone by
with husbands who once were.
Marking is such difficult work.
I unfurl my gloves to the inside out.
Sheets roar and type tames.
Buildings fall and paper remains.

FLATTENING

Salt rubs

                         my cheek,
an animal's muzzle, a wish
for relief. For   things
      set right. My daughter
and I

           living in

                     remains.

IN THE SMALL TIME

All the poems ended before this time
when poems must come, past the poem time
of making. And how making seems small,
the stitching of things that will bring beauty,
human things made
in the small time.

If we stood at our windows
and watched fear open to the street,
if we wanted to fix the broken things that
will now be taken away,
we would see the old masters, the ones who
wrote of fascism and genocide.

What is our work now? To gather,
to lift our faces from our phones.
To look up. To ask: What is the sky to us,
what is our sun to us?
What is our rising sea level to us? What of the people
who came from other countries, came to us for refuge
and work? What of them?

America, lift your faces from your phones.
Take no consolation in what you find there.
Do you see the sky? Do you walk in the forest?
Do you see the places taken to their splinters?
The friends who are fearful?
Lift your faces.

The world is upon you. Upon you with immigration
officers and clinics that turn people away.
Look for the soup kitchens. Look for gates, for golf courses.
We sold out to angry people.
And we feared they wouldn't come
until the makings formed endings
in the launching of our shouts.

I AM STILL LOOKING UP TO FIND YOU

Our city, once slow and dim, is erasing itself
from within—a weave of hoists and scaffolding,
pits of light beams and the scrape-scrape

of all that replacing—the work shovels on.
City lots pressed to dirt, cranes set on inclines,
this old apartment house diminished,

dark now in a world gone feral with all things
shiny. Through the curtain wedge: a chapel stage
where one old poet wheezes, toothless,

into a microphone. Upstairs, a woman, young,
is writing and won't look up. Six generations
before she arrived, the land was pine and

cedar on the hill, quiet in the needle-down,
the peat underfoot. Tribes gathered to the river;
salmon dried on racks and timber slid to the flats.

This building's small fate, how it ached its way
into erasure, fills again by verse and wish,
all our glimpses imploding: demolition's kiss.

THE DEMOLITION: BEFORE AND AFTER

1. On Site

Firemen came to
practice while we
watched from the park.
They flung ropes and
spun along the eaves,
shimmied to the roof
and cut trapdoors
through the shingles.

At the peak,
one lamp hung
for a long time.
A wire drooped.
The rafters held
while the maw
ate through walls.
Beams and
splinters,
tar paper crunch
as the cedar shakes
singe-crackled.
Lathe and plaster,
planks and plywood,
gutters snapped.
Insulation billowed.
The crossbeam
slipped; something
sweet
shuddered down.

2. From the Wire

GHOST GIRL: Nevermore.

DEAD POET: No ravens, please. Don't speak.

GHOST GIRL: I have to move now.

DEAD POET: Keep on in the new building. Wait and things will change.

GHOST GIRL: There is nothing to stick to here.

DEAD POET: Eventually there will be new beams and sounds and smells. Not a ruin. But it will do.

GHOST GIRL: And just hover here? Above all this?

DEAD POET: Who lets go of whom? That will tell our fate. I have other places.

GHOST GIRL: Go, then. I'll wait.

3. Aftermath

Nothing good was left.
The day came. The sun
followed. Writing was
still on the walls.
Where the river should have been
Where the river should have been,
It erased us at the shore.

The sound of fencing
raked the perimeter.
I was alone in
the rubble. They let me
through the barricade.
Keep away from that
drop-off to the cellar.
Stay off the pile's edge
just by the hole.

Things become
not much. History's
cruelest move
is the scraping by
of what we didn't know
we'd miss by starting over.
The oven gaped open
when the door broke.
Once, my little girl
cried in that room.
We saw the space left.
We saw the air.
We admired the view:
dark sutured out,
cleaned like a wound.

The problem is
we root for plot.
Show bombings
on TV and we'll
crave wartime.
Show fragments
and we'll want them
to lead up to something.

Don't we all die wanting,
blistering and doomed,
in the midst of our heirlooms?

THE REVEAL

I brought a folding chair and a jar of bourbon.
At the spectacle, we had our roles.
Mine involved day-drinking and wearing a hard hat
while a man named Bumper
ran the dozer—clearing the site as he went,
pushing debris to the property lines.
He took the building away, bit by bit; walls tipped
while clotheslines took spins
from the slide of the roof. And floors, oh! Cedar planks
snapped, antique trim, and
the hearth fell in. Windows too, warped and satin glass,
bent and broke away from
the thumbed lead frames. An old wallet tumbled from the wall.
Cabinets, open to the sun,
splintered into where the floor had been; plaster clasped
slats then ripped away
the crown of a sconce, those marooned shelves, boards
we had stacked and slid
upstairs, tossed now into bins. Our cherry trees had
grown too big to save.
One priest sang somewhere while a ghost girl waved
through the flotsam of wood.
It was the closing we never envisioned:
orderly and kind.
The more I saw—the more I leaned forward
from the chair—
the less sad it became. Truly? We had oversung.
The end detaches;
it suspends the built from the erased. After that, it freed up
our imagining and gave us
our already-haunting, soon-to-come not-so home.

THOSE WE LEFT THERE

GHOST GIRL: The men brought me here and fixed me. Made me look nicer.

DEAD POET: I had not come on my own, you see. They insisted me here long after. Stuffed and stuck my poems into the crevices of these rooms.

GHOST GIRL: How wanted you were! My life before this building had so few days. How could I know my way out? When this house goes—

DEAD POET: You can't shed a place. You can't ever go.

GHOST GIRL: I am counting on you. I need to find a space down below. Into this new, I have to burrow.

DEAD POET: Was it you who left buckets of water at the embalmer's door?

GHOST GIRL: It is hard for me to stay away, you see. I came to find out how they filled me with that grout and fluid.

DEAD POET: Ennui sent me.

GHOST GIRL: You became something. I was left in it. I was here first.

DEAD POET: And you remain so. So—

HUSBAND: How did I get mixed up in the chorus?

DEAD POET: Ah, you are new.

(DEAD) HUSBAND: How did I become part of this architecture?

GHOST GIRL: Your widow is pinning clouds to the sky-blotting.

DEAD POET: The conjuring will subside.

GHOST GIRL: And you, neither of you, will ever go.

FIXING IN PLACE WITH CURTAINS

If I could fold ~~our findings into the mouths~~
~~of the dead.~~
If I could plant ~~these souvenirs into~~
~~a poet's tomb,~~
~~into my husband's plot.~~ If I could tuck
~~what I know beneath~~
~~all things taken down.~~ If I could go back
and fix ~~one thing.~~
If I could find the country ~~where more is~~
~~less the norm.~~
If I could take ~~the memory stick and wish~~
~~it to a willow switch,~~
if I could swat ~~the longing right out of us.~~
~~Steles, corpuscles, root~~
~~matter and the clatter of people.~~ If I could
walk between clouds.
~~The little girl who lived here, twenty now,~~
~~who once laughed~~
~~and trotted across the floors,~~
~~up to the stage.~~ If I
could listen now ~~as she sang when she~~
~~was not supposed to.~~
If her father ~~would come back and~~ if we
could wave ~~her on.~~
~~Again.~~ If I could keep ~~waving.~~ If ~~he could.~~ If We.

FAREWELL FINALLY HUGO

From the demolition, everything lifts:
a stanza, gone now.
Powder. Finally, I suppose, it's a relief.

Wouldn't it, *for a hundred years, fall finally down?*
The mill, the house, or
the unrolling of the *stacks high above the town,*

collapsing now? From the stones and boards,
we push memory up.
Rubbish. Lumber. Salt. For what accumulates,

how could we not be grateful? We redact, we cut back
and always more remains.
From a city alive with cranes, longing fell around us.

What I ached for, I couldn't reach. Not my life
there, not our family
as it was. So goes the mill and the house where

memory resolves itself in gaze. The comings and goings
buried inside and
the almost-fit of it—the same way projections slip—

we lose or think we lose and mourn the old spots:
the tables, the stage—
my palm is still turned up. We love places

and have to let them go.
We are all,
and none of us, Richard Hugo.

EPILOGUE

THE ONCE-WAS BEGINNINGS
AND ENDINGS

To collapse the old and fend off the new,
that's where we started: the disruption
of disintegrating things,
keeping bits of the once-was,
our homage to the let-down
aching in the city-gone, shimmering.

What was once bardic splendor,
the lonely rot and ruins of the old mill
shaped cityscapes where syringes
sang in the dirt. To stand at the lip
of excavation, into the lit
aquarium a little girl had swum,
we each came to places washed
out in rain, sites staged to begin again.

Remember: other people have lost
whole countries. To conflate this place
with our stories is to say,
"A persona can imitate being."
If we could fold our fixed ways,
claws grasping, and head into it,
where, oh where, would be the shore?
Instead: Buildings fall and paper remains.
A borrow pit, where the house was,
a world of beloved, disappearing scrap.
And then! A nomad crossing over.

What else to do when something is dying?
Her once gone home, her finally fall
in the way down place,
stranded on the far parchment.

Memory: the harshest art
of censorship.

POET: You can't shed place.
GIRL: All of you became something.
POET: Try to reshape that into a name.
GIRL: In the midst of the heirlooms?
In the smaller of the smallest storms,
my life is left in this terrarium,
a little smelter smashing ore.
POET: Exactly that. A typewriter-on-a-plate
dilemma, flimsy in the flotsam wake.
GIRL: Demolition's kiss in the gone-by place.
Oh so impossible to erase it.

SHIFTING THE CURTAINS IN PLACE

~~If~~ I could fold ~~our findings into the mouths~~
~~of the dead.~~
~~If I could plant~~ these souvenirs into
~~a poet's tomb,~~
~~into my husband's plot. If I could tuck~~
~~what I know beneath~~
all things taken down. ~~If I could go back~~
~~and fix one thing.~~
~~If I could find the country where more is~~
~~less the norm.~~
~~If I could take the memory stick and wish~~
~~it to a willow switch,~~
~~if I could swat~~ the longing ~~right out of us.~~
~~Steles, corpuscles, root~~
~~matter and the~~ clatter ~~of people. If I could~~
~~walk between clouds.~~
~~The little girl who lived here, twenty now,~~
~~who once laughed~~
~~and trotted across the floors,~~
~~up to the stage. If I~~
~~could listen now as she~~ sang ~~when she~~
~~was not supposed to.~~
~~If her father would come back and if we~~
~~could wave her~~ on.
~~Again. If I could keep waving. If he could. If We.~~

SAY YOU COME HERE

The city is yours, dim and rain-draped—
a metropolis where what could happen
falls finally upon you and so, on a whiff
of mist, you are following
gusts pinched through the streets,
along pavement silted, grit-spat.
See that blocked-off lot?
Two huge cedars along the fence.
Take the view through broken slats:
a borrow pit, where the house was.

HERE

a borrow   house was.

SAY

house

NOTES

Erasure is not new. Artists and writers, in search of embedded stories and images, have been redacting books, images and texts for centuries. My inspiration came from Rebecca Brown's beautiful erasures and the cut-and-paste parties Matthew Stadler, Jan Wallace, and I had, along with the erasure in our city, the slipping of the new inside templates of old façades.

In conversations with his friends Lois Welch and Bill Kittredge, Hugo said, "Every house I ever lived in has been torn down."

"Façademies" is a term Lucien Pellegrin uses. Façadism is an architectural term for the same procedure.

"The practice of facadism emerged in the 1980s, when construction technology made it possible to retain a mere sliver of a frontage, and as the rise of the conservation movement increased pressure to preserve the historic streetscape—even if it didn't care much for what happened beyond the surface. It can be done well, as along Regent Street, where vastly different interiors are cleverly inserted behind regular cream-cake facades. But too often, it remains a token gesture, even a willful two fingers up to the conservation officer, facades left butchered and awkwardly marooned, as if to say: 'You made us keep it, and just see how you like it now.'"

— "Bad developments making a joke of historic buildings" Oliver Wainright, *The Guardian*, August 25, 2014.

The poems take as an inspiration Richard Hugo's great American anthem, "Degrees of Gray in Philipsburg," and his poems "Letter to Oberg from Pony" and "The Milltown Union Bar."

Seamus Heaney's poem "Clearances" inspired "What Happened There" and lines from Heaney's poem are quoted in mine.

"Where the House Was" is the title of a Richard Hugo poem. It is also the title of the film that Team Demo Hugo made.

The Frontier Room was an old bar on First Avenue in Seattle. Once a haunt of sailors and longshoremen, it became a hangout for musicians and artists in the late 1980s and early 1990s.

Lines from "Come as You Are" and "In Bloom," Nirvana songs, are in the poem "Where Did You Go, Kurt Cobain?"

"The Street Song Last on Everyone's Lips" is a quote from *One-Way Street* by Walter Benjamin.

"The Iceberg or The Ship" is a riff on Elizabeth Bishop's poem "The Imaginary Iceberg."

Roland Barthes's essay, "Paris Not Flooded" is from *Mythologies* and influenced "Practical."

Fatima Mernissi's notion of a woman being a nomad shaped the poem "Crossing Over the Crossing-Over Land." See *Dreams of Trespass*. The "Crossing-Over Place" is a translation of the Duwamish name for Seattle.

ACKNOWLEDGEMENTS

To Cali Kopczick, the finest editor a writer could ever have, my gratitude. And to the adventurous and inspiring Chin Music and its publishers Bruce Rutledge and Yuko Enomoto, I am so thankful to work with you. Thank you to Dan Shafer for your beautiful work. Thank you Erin Hoffman at Chin Music Press, too. Jan Wallace and Carmine Chickadel, thank you both for shepherding this book through vital transitions. I am truly grateful to you. Claire Summa, thank you for your early erasures—they inspired my own. And to Dara Wier, Maya Sonenberg, Wendy Feuer, Lois Welch, Margot Kenly, and Bill Cumming, thank you. Katharyne Mitchell and Matt Sparke, too. In gratitude to the Simpson Center for the Humanities at the University of Washington, Kathy Woodward, the University of Washington Honors Program and to my students. Laura Kastner and Philip Mease, thank you for staying in during ceiling floods and glass-in-the-boots sorts of events. Thank you Emer Dooley and Rob Short for giving me the grandest place to work on *Timber Curtain* Kilcrohane, on the Sheepshead Peninsula, in West Cork, Ireland. Thank you Lucky 7 Foundation, 4 Culture, Seattle Office of Arts and Cultural Affairs, and Love City Love—they all supported this project. Thank you.

CULTURE

OFFICE OF ARTS & CULTURE
SEATTLE

To *Poetry Northwest, Crab Creek Review,* and *Jubilat,* where "At the River Mouth," "Good Intentions," and "In the Small Time" (as "On Not Looking Up") appeared first.

Team Demo Hugo includes Ryan K. Adams, Wanda Bertram, Suzanne Boretz, Lucas Burdick, Jack Chelgren, Tyler DeFriece, Steve Fisk, Ananya Garg, Adria Goetz, Lori Goldston, Madeleine Greaves, Natalie Hillerson, Wayne Horvitz, Anisa Jackson, Lisa Jaech, Charlie Jones, Cali Kopczick, Ian Lucero, Frances McCue, Dandi Meng, Mara Potter, Luke Sieczek, Stephen Silha, Claire Summa, Flora Tempel...